FROM **SAND** TO **GLASS**

by Shannon Zemlicka

photographs by Randall Hyman

Lerner Publications Company / Minneapolis

The publisher thanks PPG Industries, Inc. and U.S. Silica Company for their assistance with the photographs in this book.

Lerner Publications Company
A division of Lerner Publishing Group
241 First Avenue North
Minneapolis, MN 55401 U.S.A.

Website address: www.lernerbooks.com

Library of Congress Cataloging-in-Publication Data

Zemlicka, Shannon.
    From sand to glass / by Shannon Zemlicka ; photographs by Randall Hyman
        p.   cm. — (Start to finish)
    Includes index.
    Summary: Briefly introduces the process by which glass is made from sand.
    ISBN: 0–8225–0945–8 (lib. bdg. : alk. paper)
    1. Glass manufacture—Juvenile literature. [1. Glass manufacture.] I. Title. II. Start to finish (Minneapolis, Minn.)
    TP857.3.Z46 2004
    666'.1—dc21   2002152927

Manufactured in the United States of America
1 2 3 4 5 6 – DP – 09 08 07 06 05 04

Table of Contents

Machines dig up sand 4

The sand is moved 6

The sand is dumped 8

A train moves the sand . . 10

A machine mixes
    the sand. 12

Used glass is added 14

The mix is melted 16

The glass is shaped 18

The glass is cut 20

Look out the window 22

Glossary. 24

Index 24

We can see through glass.

How is it made?

Machines dig up sand.

Glass starts as sand. Machines dig up sand from a big pit. Tiny pieces of rock called sandstone may be dug up, too. A fast stream of water breaks the sandstone into sand.

The sand is moved.

The sand is kept in big towers until a truck comes to take it away. The truck takes the sand to a building. The building has many machines that do different jobs.

The sand is dumped.

The sand may have tiny rocks in it. It is dumped on a **screen**. A screen is a piece of metal with tiny holes. The sand falls through the holes. Rocks are too big to fall through. They stay on top of the screen.

A train moves the sand.

A machine loads the sand into a train. The train takes the sand to a building where glass is made. This building is called a glass **factory**.

A machine mixes the sand.

A machine mixes the sand with soda. Soda is a white powder made from salt. The machine also mixes in a kind of crushed stone called lime. Together the sand, soda, and lime are called **mix**.

Used glass is added.

Broken glass is dumped into the mix. This glass has already been used to make things like bottles. It can be made into new glass and used again. Making something new out of something that has been used is called **recycling**.

The mix is melted.

The mix is loaded into a machine called a **furnace**. The furnace heats the mix. The mix melts. It becomes liquid glass.

The glass is shaped.

Liquid glass can be shaped into many things. This machine shapes liquid glass into a thin, flat sheet for making windows. The glass cools. It becomes hard.

The glass is cut.

The sheet of glass is much bigger than a window. A cutting machine cuts the glass. Each piece will become one window.

Look out the window.

Glass lets light in. It lets you see out. What do you see when you look outside?

Glossary

factory (FAK-tur-ee): a building where things are made

furnace (FUR-nuhs): a machine that makes heat

mix (MIHKS): sand, soda, and lime

recycling (ree-SY-klihng): making something new out of things that have been used

screen (SKREEN): a piece of metal with tiny holes

Index

digging, 4

dumping, 8, 14

melting, 16

rocks, 4, 8

sand, 4, 6, 8, 10, 12

shaping, 18

train, 10

windows, 18, 20, 22

Dad, Who Will I Be?

Dad, Who Will I Be?

Taylor Made Publishing, LLC
PO Box 20245 Greenville, NC 27858
www.taylormadenc.com

copyright # 1-2120277461

ISBN: 978-0-9965937-3-1

Editor: Jorge L. Hernandez

Printed in USA.

DEDICATION

To my son Garrett, you motivate me daily to become a better man. I know that you are destined to be better than I can ever hope to become. There is nothing you cannot do because you stand on the shoulders of giants. You are a descendant of a powerful people whose global contributions are immeasurable. I love you more than myself. You are amazing and can be whatever you want to be!

Will I be as big as a mountain or as tall as a tree?

Will I be as smart
as Garrett Morgan
or W.E.B.?

Son, you are amazing and you can be whatever you want to be.

yes, my son, you can be whatever you want to be.

Can I be as powerful as Dr. King and help the world to see that no man should rest until all the world is free?

Maybe I'll be a superhero
fighting crime wherever I see.

or a hero like Marcus Garvey, who worked to liberate you and me.

Maybe I can be an astronaut like Ronald McNair or Guion Bluford and fly in the sky farther than the eye can see.

Dad, maybe I can be the U.S. Secretary of State like Colin Powell and serve my country faithfully.

Son, you can be anything you want to be, but today I just want you to be the best YOU that YOU can be!

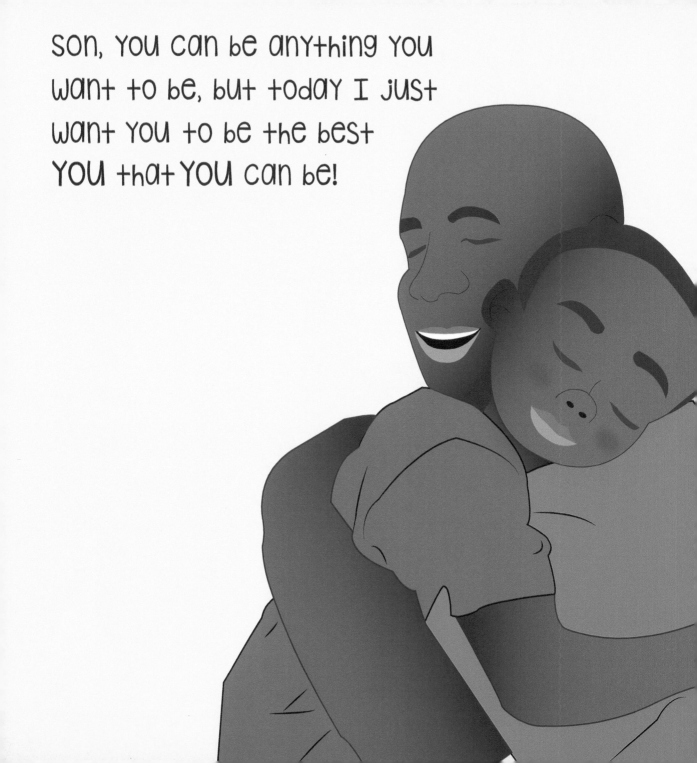

Learn More!

Parents, the following pages help you and your young scholar learn more about the amazing people mentioned in this book. I hope you enjoy reading and discovering more about each of them. **HAPPY LEARNING!**

Garrett Augustus Morgan was one of the country's most successful African-American inventors. He created two amazing inventions: the gas mask and the traffic signal. Morgan also invented a zigzag stitching attachment for manually operated sewing machines. He also founded a company that made personal grooming products, such as hair dying ointments and the curved-tooth pressing comb.

William Edward Burghardt Du Bois, better known as W.E.B. Du Bois, was the first African American to earn a Ph.D. from Harvard University. Du Bois wrote about and advocated for African-American rights during the first half of the 20th century. He co-founded the National Association for the Advancement of Colored People in 1909. Du Bois died in Ghana in 1963.

Michael Jordan is one of the greatest basketball players of all time. He was drafted by the Chicago Bulls and helped them win six championships. For his efforts, Jordan received the NBA Rookie of the Year Award, five regular-season MVPs and three All-Star MVPs. Jordan became the most decorated player in the NBA.

Muhammad Ali is an African-American boxer considered among the greatest heavyweights in the sport's history. He won his first world heavyweight championship in 1964 from Sonny Liston. Ali was an author, movie and television star and even earned a star on the Hollywood Walk of Fame. He was also a civil rights hero who spoke against war and discrimination.

Eldrick Tont "Tiger" Woods is an American professional golfer who is among the most successful golfers of all time and one of the highest-paid athletes in the world. He has been ranked number one for more weeks than any other golfer. Woods has broken numerous golf records and has many titles and championships.

The Rev. Dr. Martin Luther King Jr. was a leader in the African-American Civil Rights Movement. He is best known for his role in the advancement of civil rights using nonviolent civil disobedience. Dr. King helped to organize the 1963 March on Washington where he delivered his famous "I Have a Dream" speech. Dr. King's work lead to some of the country's most important advancements in civil rights.

Mansa (King) Abu Bakr II was the ninth mansa of the Mali Empire who left his throne in order to explore "the limits of the ocean." He led an expedition of 2,000 ships from Africa to the Americas. Evidence of his journey was found off the coast of Brazil.

Mansa Musa was the 14th-century emperor of Mali. He is regarded as the richest man in all of history. His elaborate pilgrimage to the Muslim holy city of Mecca in 1324 introduced him to rulers in the Middle East and in Europe. He gave away so much gold during his pilgrimage that he bankrupted the Egyptian economy. His leadership ensured decades of peace and prosperity in Western Africa.

Marcus Mosiah Garvey Jr. was a Jamaican political leader, publisher, journalist, entrepreneur and orator who was a staunch proponent of the Black Nationalism and Pan-Africanism movements, to which end he founded the Universal Negro Improvement Association and the African Communities League. He founded the Black Star Line, in order to help black people return to Africa.

Dr. Guion Stewart "Guy" Bluford, Jr. is an engineer, NASA astronaut and the first African American in space in 1983, as a member of the crew of the Space Shuttle Challenger on the mission STS-8. He was inducted into the International Space Hall of Fame and the United States Astronaut Hall of Fame.

Ronald Ervin McNair, Ph.D. was an African-American astronaut. McNair died on his second mission during the launch of the Space Shuttle Challenger on Jan. 28, 1986. While Ronald McNair's life was cut short, he left a legacy of excellence that endures until today.

Colin Luther Powell was the 65th United States Secretary of State and the first African American to serve in that position. General Powell also served as National Security Advisor and as Commander of the U.S. Army Forces Command. He was also the first, and so far only, African American to serve on the Joint Chiefs of Staff.

Barack Obama is the 44th President of the United States and the first African American to hold the office. President Obama is a graduate of Columbia University and Harvard Law School, where he served as president of the Harvard Law Review. He worked as a community organizer, a civil rights attorney and taught constitutional law at the University of Chicago Law School. He also served three terms representing the 13th District in the Illinois Senate.

Author G. Todd Taylor has been committed to uplifting the lives of youth for over 20 years. At an early age, he recognized the issues facing his community and has since worked diligently to solve them. His works are geared towards highlighting positive parenting and assisting youth in developing strong resiliencies to promote healthy lifestyles. Over the years, he was worked as school teacher, a counselor, an entrepreneur and a community activist. Of all the titles he has possessed, the title of DAD is the one he cherishes most.

Delayna Robbins is an Illustrator and graphic designer residing in Rocky Mount, North Carolina. She graduated from Elizabeth City State University in 2014 with a Bachelor of Science in Graphic Design. As a freelance graphic artist she specializes in illustrations and painting. Her inspirations range color theory, impressionism with abstract, and African American art. At present she is working closely with Taylor Made Publishing.

Lightning Source UK Ltd.
Milton Keynes UK
UKHW052149070519
342251UK00001B/19/P